Making a will

Making a will

by
JULIAN WORTHINGTON

foulsham
LONDON • NEW YORK • TORONTO • SYDNEY

foulsham

The Publishing House, Bennetts Close,
Cippenham, Berkshire

ISBN 0-572-02125-9

Designed and typeset by Peter Constable Consultants Ltd, London
Printed in Great Britain by Cox and Wyman Ltd, Reading, Berkshire

Contents

IT'S WHAT MUM
WOULD HAVE WANTED....

Introduction

It is a sad but inevitable fact of life that it eventually ends in death. Whether this is sudden and unexpected or drawn-out and anticipated, the grief it leaves behind can make it a particularly traumatic and difficult period for one's nearest and dearest.

Unfortunately the grief does not always stop there. The aftermath of death and all its consequences can create the most unwelcome and unwanted problems and upsets for both relatives and friends.

Certainly one way in which all of us can help minimize such potential distress is to ensure we have made a will before we die. It is, perhaps, interesting to note here that up to a third of people who die do not make a valid will.

For many, the situation may appear sufficiently straightforward and therefore not a cause for any concern. With a modest property, limited financial resources and the average range of personal possessions, what possible complications could arise?

In any event, it would all pass to the wife or husband left behind, wouldn't it?

The truth of the matter is that a lot of people underestimate the value of their possessions, while remaining blissfully ignorant of the law relating to estates in general and inheritance tax liability in particular.

It may, therefore, come as some surprise to find that there are pitfalls. And the tragedy is that these could be avoided if people thought carefully about their personal situation and prepared in advance.

This involves making all the necessary provisions and stating them clearly in a will. And the sooner this is done, the better.

The last thing people with their whole life ahead of them would want to contemplate is the question of dying - or, more accurately, what happens to the family or relatives who survive them.

But the need to draw up even the simplest of wills becomes ever more pressing as life progresses and, hopefully, fortunes advance. Success at work will bring monetary reward. Marriage will mean responsibility for others, especially where this involves children. Property purchases will increase assets. And the desire for security through insurance cover and pension plans will result in further financial benefit.

It is surely clear already, given such conditions, that one does not have to be 'rich' to leave a sizeable estate.

The purpose of this book is to guide you through the basic procedures necessary for making a valid and problem-free will - whether you do this yourself or seek professional help.

Although it is not intended to be a substitute for the knowledge and experience of a solicitor in such matters, it should create a fuller awareness of exactly what is involved and help answer most of the questions you are likely to ask.

And such information is essential for ensuring that what you want to happen on your death actually does happen.

Finally, it must be stressed that although every effort has been made to ensure that the contents of this book are accurate and correct at the time of publishing, those laws relating to wills and inheritance are always subject to change.

This applies particularly to tax liability and sizes of gifts and it is essential that you check on such areas yourself from time to time to ascertain the latest situation.

When you have read this book, we hope you will be convinced of the need to make a will - and the sooner the better.

CHAPTER 1

Can I make my own will?

If you have or own anything in the way of money, property or possessions you should make a will to ensure that those you want to benefit after your death do so without problems or disappointment.

In most cases, where individual situations are relatively straightforward, the drawing up of a will is not complicated and need not necessarily involve the services of a solicitor or legal adviser.

Provided that you follow certain basic procedures (*as described in Chapter 6*), you can write your own will, which will in its final form remain legally binding unless for any reason a court of law sees fit to change it (*see Chapter 10*).

The only other limiting factor on exactly how you dispose of what you possess - a matter over which you otherwise have total control - will be the unavoidable consideration of tax liability (*see Chapter 7*).

In principle, therefore, you are free and able

to make your own will how and when you like - with the following exceptions:

AGE

A will made by anyone under the age of eighteen (a 'minor') will **NOT** be valid unless that person is a member of the armed forces on 'active service' (*see Appendix III*).

MENTAL HEALTH

A will made by anyone who was insane at the time it was written will **NOT** be valid.

That does not mean, however, that people who are mentally ill cannot ever make a will. As long as there is good evidence that they were sane at the time it was drawn up, that will stands.

Equally a will made by someone who at a later stage is certified mentally ill remains valid.

It is usually the case that any will drawn up and witnessed correctly (*see Chapter 6*) will be judged to have been made while that person was sane, provided there is no evidence to prove otherwise.

So how does one define 'insanity'?

The condition would normally apply to anyone certified and held in a mental institution.

Also, under the Mental Health Act, it would cover someone in 'a state of arrested or incomplete development of mind which includes sub-normality of intelligence and is of such a nature or degree that the patient is incapable of living an independent life or guarding against serious exploitation'.

In any situation where there is a possibility of insanity being used as a reason to invalidate a will, a sensible precaution would be to have a qualified doctor act as a witness and to record that the person is not only capable of making the will but also understands what is in it.

That would also apply to someone old, infirm or otherwise seriously ill.

WHO CAN MAKE A WILL?

Anyone in a 'sane' condition over the age of 18

Armed forces personnel under the age of 18 if on active service

Married women with their own land or property

Prisoners with their own land or property

Foreigners with land or property in the United Kingdom, who wish it to be disposed of according to English law

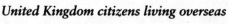 *United Kingdom citizens living overseas*

CHAPTER 2

Why should I make a will?

The simple answer is that if you want more than just your next of kin to benefit after your death from anything you own - or equally you want to impose any specific conditions on the disposal of your assets - you must make a will to ensure your wishes are carried out.

If you die without making a will - or without leaving a current one - then the law of intestacy will be applied to the distribution of your estate.

Depending on what family you have, your property is allocated in a predetermined way - after all relevant costs, such as the funeral and administration, have been settled.

SO WHO EXACTLY WILL BENEFIT?

Given certain conditions, the distribution of your estate will, in basic order of preference, be as follows:

1. Your spouse (husband or wife)

2. Your children (including illegitimate & adopted)
3. Your parents
4. Your brothers and sisters
5. Your half-brothers and half-sisters
6. Your grandparents
7. Uncles and aunts (whole blood)
8. Uncles and aunts (half blood)

(NOTE: Group 7 means your parents' brothers & sisters and Group 8 your parents' half-brothers and half-sisters.)

Bear in mind that where any of the above mentioned relatives die before you, their children would by law benefit in their place.

AND UNDER WHAT CONDITIONS?

IF   your spouse is still living

BUT   there are no children, parents, brothers or sisters (or their children) living

THEN   your spouse benefits totally

IF   your spouse is still living

AND   you have children

THEN   your estate will be divided as follows:

SPOUSE: All your personal items
+ Up to £75,000 (as available)
+ Interest at 6% from your death
+ Life interest in half the residue *

CHILDREN (in equal shares): Half the residue
+ The other half on your spouse's death

14

(* Life interest means use of rather than ownership and, in the case of money for example, involves income from any capital - not the capital itself.)

IF   your spouse is still living

AND   there are no children

BUT   there are parents, brothers and/or sisters (and/or their children) also living

THEN your estate will be divided as follows:

      SPOUSE: All your personal items

                + Up to £125,000 (as available)

                + Interest at 6% from your death

                + Half the residue

      PARENTS: Half the residue

      or (if no parents are living)

      BROTHERS/SISTERS (in equal shares):

      Half the residue

It is important to note here that your spouse is, by law, entitled to continue residing in the matrimonial home (where he or she was living when you died).

IF   there is no spouse living

BUT   there are children

THEN your estate will be divided between them in equal shares when they are 18 or marry (whichever occurs first)

IF   there is no spouse living
AND   no children
BUT   there are parents living
THEN your estate will be divided between them
         in equal shares

IF   there is no spouse living
AND   no children
AND   no parents
THEN your estate will be divided (in equal
         shares) between:
         BROTHERS/SISTERS or if none
         HALF-BROTHERS/HALF-SISTERS
         or if none
         GRANDPARENTS or if none
         UNCLES/AUNTS (whole blood) or if none
         UNCLES/AUNTS (half blood)

AND WHAT ARE THE PROBLEMS?

Although the law of intestacy is designed to cover all normal situations, there are some circumstances not included which may be relevant. For example:

DIVORCE

A divorced person has no right of entitlement to any part of the estate of a former spouse who has died - as from the time of the decree absolute.

SEPARATION

There is an important distinction here between a separation order granted by a Divorce Court and a Magistrates' Court order concerning separate habitation. In the former case, there is no entitlement. In the latter, there is as normal for a living spouse.

COHABITATION

Under the law of intestacy, if you were living with someone (but not married) at the time of your death, that person has no direct entitlement to benefit from your estate. Any claim, therefore, would have to be made under the Inheritance (Provision for Family and Dependants) Act 1975 *(see Chapter 10)*.

In the average situation, of course, it may well be that you are quite happy for your estate to be distributed according to the law of intestacy. If this is the case, then you would be well advised to draw up a brief will to this effect *(see Chapter 6)*, if only to clarify the position.

Any deliberate decision to die intestate must, however, be carefully considered against what exactly your estate consists of and ultimately whom you want to benefit from it.

CHAPTER 3

When should I make a will?

While in no way wishing to sound morbid, there is no time like the present to make your will. After all, none of us knows what might happen tomorrow!

Seriously, though, it is a sensible precaution to make a will regardless of years, health or circumstance. Particularly in this day and age, it is often surprising to reflect how much individuals are actually worth.

For example, you may own your own property - as is the case with the majority of people now, whether solely or jointly. That in itself is a sizeable asset.

Perhaps you may not have that much money in the bank. But have you considered the value of your savings, life or other insurance policies, maybe even some investments such as shares? Even amongst your personal possessions, there could be some items worth more than you think, such as antique furniture or jewellery.

Just because you may not have a large bank balance does not mean that you are not worth anything in financial terms. And it may well be that there are others, apart from your immediate family, that you would like to help, should the situation arise.

Here are just some examples of possible changes in your personal situation that could well justify the making of a will.

- Marriage
- Property
- Children
- Divorce
- Travel
- Illness
- Employment
- Financial success
- Inheritance

MARRIAGE

In the euphoria of your wedding day, the possibility or occasion of your death will certainly be the last thing on your mind. However, you should not forget the additional responsibilities you are assuming or the wisdom of making certain provisions.

Bearing in mind what your spouse would be entitled to if you were to die intestate *(see Chapter 2)*, it would be sensible to make it clear from the start exactly what you want your partner to have.

One point worth remembering here is that marriage in itself will automatically revoke any existing will *(see Chapter 9)*, although not in Scotland *(see Appendix II)*. If you wish to retain any of your previous bequests, you should certainly make another will at this time.

PROPERTY

As we have already mentioned, property is probably most people's major asset in terms of value. At the time of purchase, whether or not you happen to be married, it would be a wise precaution to make a simple will, in which you should include whom you wish to benefit from such an asset in the event of your death.

CHILDREN

Under the law of intestacy *(see Chapter 2)*, any children you have will automatically benefit after your death. And this includes all illegitimate and legally adopted children.

This means that under normal circumstances your offspring would be provided for, whether or not you had made a will.

However, it is a sensible precaution to clarify exactly how and when they might benefit, particularly as they grow up and situations change - for example, with their own marriage.

Equally, while they are still very young, you

may decide to leave everything to your spouse and let her (or him) make a decision at a later date.

Whatever the case may be, it is sensible to set out your wishes in a will. Of course, you are free to change this at any time.

DIVORCE

Here again, it is important to remember what the law of intestacy states *(see Chapter 2)*. If you die without leaving a will, then your divorced spouse loses all rights to claim any part of your estate.

You may, of course, be quite happy with this situation. However, if you do wish your divorced spouse to benefit in any way, then you must make a will in which you state clearly exactly what you want her (or him) to have. The situation is the same where a married couple have been legally separated.

According to the law, any children by this or a previous marriage would still benefit. But you may well wish to clarify your exact wishes in relation to all or any of your children under these circumstances.

TRAVEL

Without wishing to imply that travel is a particularly dangerous occupation or that it carries a high mortality risk, for those who go abroad, particularly on a regular basis, the making of a will would be a sensible precaution.

Although statistics have shown that it is safer to fly than to cross the road, the more time you spend in transit, the more you will increase the chances of becoming one of the fortunately rare exceptions.

This becomes even more relevant should you happen to be going into or through any of the world's 'trouble spots'.

ILLNESS

Just because you fall ill does not mean, of course, that you are likely to die. And with the advances in modern medecine and operation techniques, most people recover from the most serious of conditions.

However, where there are incidents or a history of serious illness - even hereditary problems, it would be sensible to be prepared in advance of that possibly fatal event. And, if you leave it too late, you may not be in a fit condition to make your will.

EMPLOYMENT

Certain occupations carry a much higher risk of accident, injury or illness than others. You yourself will know whether your work comes within this category. If not, you only have to check it out with an insurance company.

For the sake of your family and others you

would want to benefit from your estate in the unlikely event of something happening in the course of your daily work or duties, it would be sensible to make a will - just in case.

FINANCIAL SUCCESS

Another aspect of your working life that could advance the decision to make a will is that of success. The more you earn, the more you will have to leave to others when you die. And, as a consequence, the more complicated your estate may become.

One important aspect here is tax *(see Chapter 7)* and you should be constantly aware of your enhanced financial situation and plan accordingly to ensure you pass on the maximum benefit to others.

The same would also apply should you ever be lucky enough to win sizeable amounts of money or other items of particular value.

INHERITANCE

Yet another occasion when it would be wise to consider the future and take the necessary steps to protect your good fortune is following an inheritance.

Should you be the happy beneficiary of sizeable amounts of money or property, then you in turn should make the necessary arrangements for those you would like to benefit after your death.

THE LAST WILL...

In all the examples mentioned here, it is of course possible and, in many cases, likely that your personal situation will change over time.

Should you, for example, make a will when you are twenty, then you would almost certainly need to alter or adjust it by the time you reach forty, when possibly you are married with children, own property and enjoy an enhanced position in your working life.

There is no problem here. You can - and should - change your will as your circumstances change (see Chapter 9). Just because you make one will does not mean that it is cast in stone for the rest of your life. You can alter - or preferably rewrite it - as often as you like.

CHAPTER 4

What can I put in my will?

The principle purpose of a will is to ensure that everything you own is disposed of in the way you would wish. This means that the main content would include all money, property and personal items you want to pass on - to family, friends, associates, organizations or charities, for example.

There are, of course, other aspects you may wish to mention, such as what you want done with your body and any specific arrangements you would like made with regard to your funeral.

You may also wish to make some general statements (known as recitals) expressing special sentiments or intentions.

These will be covered later in the chapter.

The main areas to consider include:
- Money
- Buildings
- Land

- Insurance policies
- Shares
- Trusts
- Personal items

MONEY

It is not, of course, necessary to specify gifts of money, which incidentally are called pecuniary legacies, in your will. Quite often - and particularly where there may not be much in the way of actual cash - this would normally come within the estate itself.

However, you may want to leave certain sums to people who would otherwise not benefit - perhaps relatives, friends or those who have worked for you - as a goodwill gesture. Such bequests would have to be spelt out.

Money here covers all amounts held in current and savings accounts in banks or other financial institutions. And it is important that you leave all relevant information easily to hand in the event of your death to save problems afterwards over tracing what money you have and where or with whom it is held *(see Appendix IV)*.

BUILDINGS

If you own your own house or flat, then you are of course entitled to leave this in your will. It may well be that you in fact own more than one property, in which case you should include all of them. The only other relevant condition is that you are the SOLE owner.

Where any property is in joint names as 'beneficial joint tenants' (as opposed to 'tenants in common' - most usually husband and wife), then you are not entitled to dispose of your share. This would automatically pass to the other joint owner - or owners, where there are more than two - on your death.

It may well be that, after making a will, your situation changes. For example, you might purchase another property or, indeed, sell one. Remember to make the necessary adjustments to the original will.

This is also important where you are the joint owner of one or several properties and the other parties involved die before you. In this situation, you are entitled - as sole surviving beneficial joint owner - to dispose of those properties as you wish.

It is also possible to leave property that you do not own, but of which you have the leasehold. This situation is particularly relevant to flats. It should be noted, however, that in some cases it is necessary to gain the consent of the owner before assigning the lease. On your death, the responsibility for this would fall to your executor.

LAND
Similar principles apply to land as to

buildings. In most cases the two are combined. It could be, however, that you own land which does not form part of any residence. This would apply, for example, to agricultural land. Anything on that land, such as farm buildings, animals or crops would normally form part of the bequest, unless you were to stipulate otherwise.

FOREIGN PROPERTY

This can be a difficult area, since normally any property you own abroad that you wish to dispose of will be covered by the laws of that country.
If you are in this situation you should seek legal advice.

INSURANCE POLICIES

You should check carefully the terms of any insurance policy you hold since it may well be that there are certain restrictions as to who can benefit from any money payable on your death. It could be, for example, that particular people are specified - such as the spouse or, in the case of equity against a loan or other borrowings, a bank or other financial institution. If not, then you can bequeath any money due on your death.

SHARES

Normally shares can be bequeathed in a will just like other property or possessions that you own. However, it is possible that there are restrictions as to how these can be dealt with. One example of this could be shares held in a private company.

TRUSTS

These can be set up for the benefit of members of your family or for charitable purposes and there are certain advantages to be gained, particularly over the question of tax, where estates are large enough to incur financial penalties.

But the organization of trusts is a complex issue and you would be ill-advised to attempt this on your own. Professional advice is really essential here.

PERSONAL ITEMS

You are, of course, entitled to leave specific items or possessions in your will and there is in some cases a definite advantage in doing this. But you should be clear that such legacies are separate from those of money - or land.

The difference is an important one if you should, by chance, have bequeathed more in your will than you actually own.

The law is quite clear on this point. Where you have insufficient funds to pay for outstanding debts or the costs and expenses incurred by your death, then whatever money that can be retrieved will be - from any financial gifts you have stipulated. Personal items, such as jewellery or other objects of value, cannot be touched IF you have clearly identified these in your will.

To clarify this point, it is not sufficient to state in your will that "I leave all my jewellery" or "all my antique silver". You must specify individual items or sets of items.

To avoid any problems with this or any other part of your material bequests, you should of course make sure you don't try to leave more than you have!

 GIFTS AND THE TAX MAN

It is important to remember that under certain circumstances gifts can be taxable.
Details on the principles of when and where tax may be payable are included in Chapter 7.

YOUR FUNERAL

Although not a subject anyone would wish to dwell on, the question of how you wish your body to be disposed of after your death and any specific details about the ceremony are almost certainly matters you will have already discussed with your next of kin, be it your spouse or a near relative, or possibly a very close friend.

It is also quite common practice to include such details in your will, although it may be that funeral arrangements are finalized before the contents of your will are generally made known to those concerned.

Ideally you should do both, which means making sure beforehand that someone knows what you would like to happen. One way of doing this is to write down your wishes in the form of a letter and give this to your executor so that any instructions can be carried out with the minimum of delay.

The kind of information relevant would be the type of ceremony you wanted, depending on your religion, and any specific details such as hymns to be sung or music played. You could stipulate where this was to be held and whether you wanted to be buried or cremated. You might even want to detail the type of gravestone or where you wished your ashes to go.

There is normally no reason why any reasonable instructions you leave should not be carried out. However they are not legally binding, since the law does not recognize a body as property. This means that your executors are entitled to make the final decision, even if this overrides your expressed wishes.

LOOKING AFTER THE GRAVE

If you decide to have a grave, tombstone or possibly even a monument or other memorial and you want to make sure that someone will look after it, you can stipulate this in your will.

This would involve either the relevant burial or local authority, whose agreement must be sought in order to carry out such maintenance. There is no obligation on the authority concerned to do this and, in any event, there is a time limit of 99 years.

YOUR BODY

You might decide to leave your body for medical research or donate certain organs. This can be done during your final illness, again in writing or in front of a minimum of two witnesses.

The need to respond immediately following your death is obvious. So you must make sure someone else knows about this. By the time your will is read, it will almost certainly be too late to save particular organs.

As far as research is concerned, the situation is similar to that of funeral arrangements. Despite your own wishes, it is possible for your spouse or next of kin to stop this happening and to request burial or cremation instead.

DONATING YOUR BODY OR ORGANS

If you decide to donate specific organs or allow your body to be used for further medical research, contact your local doctor or hospital for more details as to how this can be arranged.

MAKING A RECITAL

As we have already mentioned, you can use your will not just to ensure that your property and possessions are passed on in the way you want but also to make general statements or personal observations.

Although this is not a particularly common habit, it does provide you with the opportunity to explain why you have drawn up the will in the way you did - should this be necessary.

A word of warning, however, is necessary here.

While perhaps you feel that, by making certain statements, you will remove any possible misunderstanding among those who may or may not benefit as a result, you could run the risk of introducing ambiguities or confusion. The essence of an effective and trouble-free will is that it is absolutely clear what your intentions are - within the law, of course.

There are, at the same time, good reasons for making supplementary comments - for example, to clarify particular circumstances that exist. This could include the transfer of authority to a named person, where you have been given the power to effect something or appoint someone else to do so. Equally, you may feel it necessary to confirm a particular bequest that might otherwise be open to an element of doubt or surprise.

The most likely reason for a general statement would probably be where you wish to put on record your feelings towards a person (or people) who will not benefit directly from your will, but of whom you wish to make recognition. This could include a loyal employee or particularly good friend, where you feel they deserve special mention by way of gratitude.

CHAPTER 5

Who can I name in my will?

The answer to this lies more in the exceptions than the rule. To simplify matters, it is probably best to divide the list into individuals and groups (or institutions), since there are a number of restrictions specific to each category which you will have to take into account before naming beneficiaries.

NAMING INDIVIDUALS

In principle, you can name whom you like in your will. What exactly they can receive and when depends on a range of different circumstances existing at the time of your death.

The following should help to clarify the position in law:

ADULTS

With the exceptions or under the conditions mentioned below, any person over the age of 18 can benefit from any bequest you make in your will.

HOWEVER...

If that person dies before you OR cannot be traced within a period of seven years after your death, then the gift you made is included in the residue of the estate, that is what is left after all the various bequests have been met.

SO...

If that should happen and you want to ensure that the bequest does not become part of the residue, you should make the necessary provision for another named person to benefit in his or her place.

BUT...

If the bequest is to your children or other direct descendants and they should die before you, then the gift will automatically go to their children UNLESS you stipulate otherwise in your will. This applies equally to illegitimate children.

ALSO...

If you have made a gift to two or more people as joint owners and one of them dies, then that share is automatically passed to the other joint owner - or owners.

WITNESS BEWARE

When you ask someone to witness your will, which you must do in order to make it valid (see Chapter 6), bear in mind that they are NOT entitled to benefit from any part of that will. Nor, for that matter, is their spouse or anyone who could normally claim through them, EXCEPT...

if the bequest is in payment of a debt owing to them
OR
if they are charged to hold a gift on trust
OR
if they have only witnessed a codicil (see Chapter 9) which does not involve them
OR
if there are two other witnesses who are not benefiting from the will.

CHILDREN

You are entitled to leave what gifts you like to your own children, which incidentally includes any illegitimate child or one who has been legally adopted before the date you made your only or last will. If you have stepchildren and wish to bequeath anything to them, you should stipulate 'stepchildren' in your bequest.

There are, however, a couple of important restrictions relating to the age of your children.

If any are under eighteen - that is to say, a minor - then they are not able to own property or land. One solution here is to put the property or land in the hands of trustees until the child or children concerned reach eighteen.

In any case, you may feel that because of the value of your gift you would rather it went to your children when they were a bit older and more responsible. You can do this by setting up a trust and stating exactly the age or conditions under which the gift can be passed to them.

This introduces the other main restriction - that no child under eighteen can be a trustee.

FOREIGNERS

In principle, there is no problem about naming a national of another country as a beneficiary in your will. However the law does state that if that country is at war with your own, that person cannot receive your gift - until peace is declared. This would also apply to anyone living in such a country or in one that was under enemy occupation.

BANKRUPTS

You may find yourself in a position where you want to make a gift to someone who is either threatened with bankruptcy or already bankrupt or is running a serious risk of becoming so. The danger here is that your gift could end up in the hands of that person's creditors.

To avoid this, you can use a device known as a protective trust, which will enable the beneficiary to enjoy the interest from your gift during the period you stipulate for the trust to operate.

At the end of this period, the trustees would be empowered to distribute the gift, at their discretion, among that person and/or his family depending on the circumstances existing at that time. In any event, no creditor would benefit.

As you have probably already gathered, the setting-up of such a trust is not a particularly straightforward option. If you wish to consider it, then you should certainly seek professional advice.

MENTAL PATIENTS

There is nothing in law to prevent a person suffering with a mental illness from receiving a gift in a will, regardless of his or her state of mind. It may be that the person involved is incapable of handling that gift, in which case someone else may have to look after it on his or her behalf.

ANIMALS

You can leave money to animals, which usually would involve your pets, for their care and welfare. However, there is a time limit involved - currently 21 years.

NAMING GROUPS

In the standard will, of course, most if not all gifts are made to individuals - that is, to surviving members of the family. However it may be that you have no immediate family or possibly you decide that your estate is sufficiently large that you wish to spread some of the benefit elsewhere.

The principle of leaving money, property or possessions to groups or institutions presents no problem from a judicial point of view. But if you want to ensure the maximum benefit from such gifts to the parties concerned, you need to be aware of what the law regards as 'charitable', since there are significant tax concessions at stake.

CHARITABLE ADVICE

While this book can offer some guidelines and quote obvious examples, the question of charities is generally acknowledged as a tricky one and you should certainly seek professional advice if you are considering making such gifts in your will.

CHARITIES

It is quite common practice to leave a gift, usually money, to favourite charities. And where these are well-known and well-established, there are normally no problems. In fact, the major ones are well organized to benefit from people's bequests and will supply a special form for this purpose on request.

If, however, you chose a smaller and more obscure charity, there is always a possibility that for some reason this might cease its activities. It is a wise precaution to include an alternative in your will or make it clear that this particular gift should be for 'charitable purposes'. Its allocation would then be the responsibility of your executors.

The important point to make here is that if, for any reason, the gift cannot be passed to your chosen charity and there is no other relevant instruction, then that gift is included in the residue of your estate and could be liable for tax (*see Chapter 7*).

As very general guidelines, a gift within the following categories could under the right circumstances be regarded as 'charitable':

- Help for the aged
- Help for the disabled
- Help for the poor
- Help for the sick
- Help for the community
- Education
- Religion
- Animal welfare

It is most important to stress that the above list is highly simplified and in no way comprehensive. The key point to bear in mind is that 'charity' generally implies gifts to groups of people rather than individuals. In any event, you should seek professional advice before making any 'charitable' bequest.

BUT EXACTLY WHO ARE THE "LITTLEHAMPTON LEAGUE AGAINST WOMBAT ABUSE"?

CHAPTER 6

How do I write my will?

Probably the most important aspect of any will is how it is prepared and worded, since it must comply with certain minimum legal requirements and be free of any ambiguity.

If not, your wishes may not be carried out in exactly the way you wanted and, at worst, the will could be rejected in its entirety. As a result, your estate would be treated as if you had made no will (*see Chapter 2*).

Having said that, you should not be deterred from preparing your own will, since the formalities are relatively straightforward and the advice given in this book should help ensure that you make your bequests clearly and unambiguously.

An obvious comment, but one that needs to be stressed, is that when the time comes to administer your will, you are not going to be there to clarify any points or give any explanations. So make sure nothing you have written is open to possible interpretation or doubt.

THE ACID TEST

The best way to ensure that your intentions are perfectly clear is to get a third party to read through your will and to give you their interpretation. If this is the same as your own, then you have almost certainly achieved your objective. If not, you must look again at the problem areas.

Before you sit down to write your will, there are certain key aspects to be considered - and remembered. Although they may not seem that important to you, they could make all the difference to your intended beneficiaries! These will be explained under the following:

- Preparation
- Presentation
- Wording
- Content
- Additional documents
- Amendments
- Signature
- Witnesses

PREPARATION

Unless you want to write the simplest of wills, for example leaving everything to your spouse, then it is very important that you give yourself plenty of time for reflection.

Nothing you may decide to include in your will is cast in stone and you can, of course, rewrite it at any time. But should you die suddenly and unexpectedly, it will be too late for second thoughts.

Changes in circumstance cannot be foreseen and certainly should not be presumed in case they do not come about. However, you should make every effort to ensure that, at the time of writing, all your wishes are clearly expressed.

This is unlikely to be a five-minute job, particularly if your possessions are numerous, your finances diverse and you decide to name more than your immediate family as beneficiaries.

The best way to ensure nothing and no-one has been missed is to make some notes, reflect on these over a period of time and add to or change them as necessary.

These notes should include:

PROPERTY AND POSSESSIONS

Here you should jot down all the details of what you own in the way of buildings and land, what money you have in ALL your accounts, what savings exist in terms of insurance policies and shares and what there is in the way of personal possessions, particularly jewellery and antiques and other items of relative value.

Alongside all these entries in your list, you should put down the current value, where this can be easily assessed, or a reasonable estimation. Equally, you should include details of any amounts currently owing, such as loans (for example, mortage or hire purchase agreements) or other borrowings (such as overdrafts).

There are two very good reasons for doing this. One is to make sure you do not try to give away more than you actually have. The other is to ascertain whether your estate is of sufficient value as to incur any tax liability, which could obviously affect how you finally prepare and word your will (*see Chapter 7*).

One more important note to make here is the approximate cost of any funeral arrangements and an allowance for expenses incurred in the administration of your will. These - and any debts you have - must be deducted from your capital before you begin to allocate any sums of money.

BENEFICIARIES

Make a list of all the people you want to leave something to when you die. Here you should include any charities you wish to benefit and even your pets, should you feel this is necessary.

Alongside each entry, detail what exactly

you want to leave, be it property, money and/or personal possessions.

MAKE IT CLEAR

Although there should be little doubt over the exact identity of property or land and certainly no argument where sums of money are quoted, insufficient detail on personal possessions can lead to much disappointment.

Where you mention specific items, there must be no doubt in anyone's mind as to exactly which items you are referring. Hence a 'gold ring', 'antique table' or 'landscape painting' would almost certainly prove insufficient identification and you should include more precise descriptions.

If you think there is a need to make over any bequest in the form of a trust, note it down and decide who will act as trustees - with their permission, of course!

As far as charities are concerned, contact them for all the necessary details, including any special forms and their suggested legacy clause to be put in your will.

Once this list is completed, you must

double-check the bequests you have made against the items you included as your property and possessions. It must certainly not exceed the latter and, in terms of money, should reflect a sufficient residue to meet any tax liability, possible costs and other unspecified expenses.

RECITALS

If you want to include any general statements in your will, for example to express gratitude to anyone who will not otherwise benefit from your estate, make a note of those involved and what exactly you wish to say.

MR. CRIPPEN
JUNIOR PARTNER

CHOOSING EXECUTORS

The function of an executor is to look after the administration of your will and to ensure that your wishes as expressed in it are carried out as far as is legally possible (see 'Glossary of Terms' below).

To avoid any possible problems should all executors named in your will refuse to act in this capacity, it is best to ask them first.

It is common practice to approach members of your family, relatives or close friends to perform this role. You can use a solicitor or your bank, but remember that they will charge for their services. If you take this option, you should find out their fees and provide for payment in your will.

If the executors' services are unpaid, it would be a thoughtful gesture to leave them something in your will, unless of course they are already among the beneficiaries. They are, however, entitled to draw from your estate reasonable expenses incurred through their function.

Although a single executor is sufficient, it is a wise precaution to appoint at least two in case one should be unable or unwilling to fulfil the necessary duties.

Such preparation might seem unnecessarily tedious and time-consuming. But it is really vital if you want to ensure that your will is comprehensive and embraces all your particular wishes and, most importantly, is effected without any problems or embarrassment.

Certainly the time and effort taken in first planning what exactly you want to include in your will is going to save much aggravation caused by constant rewriting later.

PRESENTATION

You have a choice here of writing your will on sheets of paper (in fact, you can do it on any material) or filling in a printed will form, which you can obtain through good stationers or bookshops.

WRITING ON PAPER

A will can be hand-written, typed or printed - and can contain a combination of the three. While you are unlikely to want to go to the expense of having it printed, you might decide to have it typed and possibly add elements by hand. The choice is yours.

The main danger of hand-writing your will is that parts of it may not be legible and therefore would become invalid. Obviously this will depend on the individual. If you do choose to write it by hand, then make sure all of it can be read.

You can use either ink or pencil, but never mix the two. If you do, the pencilled parts will be regarded as indications of additions or changes rather than definite intentions and, as such, will be ignored.

USING A FORM

You may find the special form easier to work with, particularly if your will is straightforward. And some even contain helpful instructions to guide you through the various parts.

Basically the form has printed on it all the main legal phrases and statements necessary, with blanks spaces under each. Here you should fill in the required information or details, either by hand or typed.

It may be that some sections are not relevant in your situation. You can leave these spaces blank. For security reasons, however, you would be wise to draw a line through them to prevent the possibility of something being written there without your knowledge.

Equally, you may find that insufficient space has been allowed for everything you want to say within a particular section. In this situation, simply continue on a separate sheet of paper, but make sure you sign this at the bottom and get it witnessed *(see page 68)*.

WHAT IF I'M UNABLE TO WRITE?

*You may unfortunately not be in a position
to write your own will. It could be that you
are seriously ill or suffer some disability, such
as blindness or illiteracy, that prevents you
from doing so.*

*Whatever the reason, you can get someone else to
do this for you - and even sign it on your behalf.
The critical factor is that there is clear evidence
that you are aware of the contents.*

*This can be done by having the will read over
to you and by making sure a statement is
included at the end to the effect that you were
read all the content and you understood
and agreed it.*

*As usual, the will has to be witnessed by two
people, one of whom can write and sign on
your behalf. In the majority of such cases,
however, the person involved is normally quite
capable of signing or making his or her own
mark where appropriate.*

WORDING

It is impossible to over-stress the importance of wording your will clearly, accurately and consistently.

Apart from some standard legal expressions that it is customary to use *(see page 69)*, you are free to express your wishes in your own way. But be careful to avoid complicated phrases or expressions or too much elaboration or 'dressy' language.

The simpler the content of the will and the language used, the less chance there is for misunderstanding or confusion - and hence the possibility of some bequests being judged invalid.

If you are not sure about the exact meaning or use of a word, consult the Oxford Dictionary, since this will be the normal reference in cases of doubt.

Equally, bear in mind that words will normally be assumed to have the same meaning wherever they appear in the will, unless the content makes a possible alternative meaning clear.

GLOSSARY OF TERMS

It is obviously impossible to give a comprehensive list of words that could be used in a will. Here we have included those that refer specifically to people commonly mentioned in wills, with a brief explanation of the legal interpretation and their functions where applicable. Additionally, there are some useful and significant terms and what they mean.

One very important point to stress here is that where you mention any person in your will, always give the full names and the exact relationship to you where relevant. NEVER leave people's identity in doubt.

BENEFICIARY
This is the general term used for a person (or persons) who is named to benefit by a gift in your will.

BEQUEATH
The word is used when giving anything other than land or property. If the gift comprises land or property, then the word 'devise' is used. Thus a testator 'bequeaths' a car or sum of money, but 'devises' a house.

CHILDREN

Remember that this covers legitimate, illegitimate and legally adopted children. You should state 'stepchildren' where applicable, although this will be inferred if they are the ONLY children alive when you make your will. The same applies to grandchildren, although again it is best to specify this to avoid any confusion.

DESCENDANTS

This refers to children 'down the line' indefinitely and one way of limiting this is to specify something like 'living at my death'. The phrase 'per stirpes' should be used where you want children to benefit only in the event that their parents, as beneficiaries, die before you. Another point to remember is that where you stipulate 'descendants', all will benefit in equal shares.

DEVISE

The word is used when giving land or property. See 'Bequeath' above.

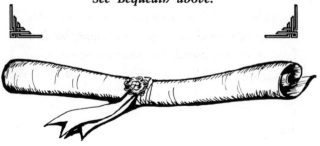

EXECUTOR

We have already mentioned the role of the executor (see 'Choosing Executors' above). Incidentally, the female version is an executrix. Whom you choose to perform this function is down to you, although minors and people certified mentally incapable are excluded.

You can nominate as many executors as you want. However, since they need to get together at some stage to administer your will, for practical reasons you should limit the number. Two is probably the norm.

And don't forget that 'professionals' will normally charge for their services and their agreement must be sought when making your will. Since no-one can charge fees unless specified in the will, they will insist that you provide for this.

FAMILY

This word has in the past led to considerable confusion and misinterpretation and should be avoided at all costs.

HUSBAND

Hardly a word one would think was open to interpretation, but there is an important qualification to be made here and that concerns divorce. In the eyes of the law, a man officially remains the husband until the decree absolute - and not the decree nisi. The effect of a divorce is to annul those parts of the will that refer directly to a previous spouse - for example, as a beneficiary or appointed executor or trustee. So, if you wish a former spouse to benefit from your will, you must stipulate this.

FREE OF TAX

Any capital transfer tax payable on a gift normally comes out of the gift or is paid by the beneficiary. For example, if tax at £50 is payable on a pecuniary legacy of £1000, the beneficiary would receive £950. If the gift was 'free of tax', the beneficiary would receive the full £1000, with the tax being paid from the residue of the estate.

ISSUE

Basically this is the same as 'descendants', but occasionally has been held to have a different meaning. The word 'issue' is well avoided by experienced will-drafters since confusion may arise.

MINOR

This refers to someone under eighteen, as does the word 'infant'. Remember that minors cannot own property or land until they become 'of age'. Any gift of this kind - and possibly large sums of money - can be put in trust for the relevant period.

NEPHEW

To save any confusion, it is always best to include the full name of any such beneficiary and his precise relationship.
As with children generally, the term applies to illegitimate nephews, as well.

NEXT OF KIN

A common expression which basically refers to your closest relation by blood.

NIECE

Here, the same advice and comments are relevant as for nephews.

PECUNIARY LEAGACY

This term is used to describe a gift of cash.

RESIDUE

What is left after payment of all the specific legacies and devises.

SURVIVOR
This word is normally used to refer to those who, at the time of your will or your death, have not yet been born.

TESTAMENTARY EXPENSES
These are the expenses of administering the estate, for example those of the executors and lawyers and the costs of advertising to trace beneficiaries, etc.

TESTATOR
This is the word used for the person making the will.

BACK TO WORK LADS,
IT WAS A
MISUNDERSTANDING.

TRUSTEE

As mentioned earlier, this is someone you 'trust' to look after particular bequests in your will on behalf of another person. Usually this occurs because the beneficiary is too young (see 'Minor') or there may be other exceptional circumstances under which you feel your gift needs protecting for a period of time - for example, in the case of a bankrupt or spendthrift. The trustee gains no benefit from the gift, but has the authority to increase the value of that gift. In the case of money, for example, the trustee can arrange for it to be invested and pass the interest on to the beneficiary. To avoid problems should the trustee die, it is normal to appoint two - at least. Because of the nature of their responsibility, they must be people in whom you have full confidence. And they cannot be minors. A final point. As with executors, if you choose 'professionals', they will require payment for their services.

WIFE

In principle, this term is self-evident. However, the same applies for a wife as for a husband in the event of divorce.

CONTENT

We have already looked at the sorts of things you can include in your will *(Chapter 4)*. When it comes to writing everything down formally, there is a recognized format and procedure you should follow to ensure the authenticity and legality of the document. This includes the obligatory insertion of certain paragraphs *(see page 69)*.

The following list should act as a useful guide to make sure that, as far as the content is concerned, you do not miss out anything essential or important.

- You MUST begin the document by stating that it is your last will and testament.
- You MUST then include your full names and address and the date on which you are writing the will.
- You MUST then state that you revoke all former wills and declare this to be your last will.
- You MUST then appoint your executors - and trustees where applicable - not forgetting to include the necessary provision for payment where relevant.
- You can, if you feel it necessary, then appoint solicitors to handle the estate (with, of course, provision for their payment).

- You should here include any instructions as to your funeral and how you wish your body to be disposed of.
- You can then make specific provision for the payment of 'testamentary expenses' - that is, administration costs such as executors' expenses, those involved in tracing beneficiaries or incidental costs arising from legal advice or disputes.
- You can also make provision for the payment of any inheritance tax where this is not already covered *(see Chapter 7)*.
- You may then wish to express your gratitude or similar sentiments to people not included in your bequests - a tactful introduction to the list of beneficiaries to follow.
- You should now provide full details of the disposal of your estate, including property and land (which you 'give and devise') and money and specific personal items (which you 'give and bequeath'), although the word 'give' is quite sufficient.
- You should also allow for any residue, after all the gifts have been allocated and expenses and costs paid, by naming a beneficiary for whatever might remain.
- You MUST finally sign your will in the presence of two witnesses, who MUST also sign against a statement to the effect that they were present together and that they can verify your signature *(see pages 67 and 68)*.

THE THIRTY-DAY CLAUSE

In the unlikely event of your immediate or sole beneficiary - for example, your spouse - dying within days of your own death, the situation could arise whereby the gifts you made passed elsewhere contrary to your wishes.

If she had not made a will, then everything you left her would automatically go to her relations.

To prevent this happening, you can make a provision in your will stipulating another beneficiary should you wife not survive you by thirty days.

STATUTORY WILL FORMS

One way of cutting down on the amount of work involved in writing your will is by using one or more of the 'statutory will forms'.

These should not be confused with the forms from stationers that you can fill in. Rather, they are existing legal documents expressing general intentions to which you can make reference in your will.

As such, they provide an effective 'shorthand' where you would otherwise need to spell out specific instructions or include a long list of personal items as a gift.

For example, 'Form 2' enables you to give all your personal possessions to someone without having to identify each and every item. Thus, you simply have to refer to the gift under 'Form 2 of the Statutory Will Forms, 1925'. Equally, 'Form 4' involves gifts to charities and can make life a lot easier for all concerned.

If you feel such forms might be useful when drawing up your will, you should seek professional advice on their exact content and use.

THE INTERNATIONAL WILL

There is now provision for someone who has property in several different countries to make one will and to have it administered in any country that is party to the convention.

And this can be done regardless of where the will was drawn up, where the assets exist or even the nationality or residence of that person.
There are, however, certain minimum requirements, as follows:

- The will must be in writing, though not necessarily that of the person making it, and can be in any language.
- The person making the will must declare in front of a solicitor and two witnesses that the document is really his/her will and that he/she is aware of its contents.
- The person making the will must then sign it (or verify his signature) at the end, as well as signing and numbering each page, in the presence of the solicitor and witnesses, who must also sign at the end.
- The solicitor must add the date of the signing at the end, which effectively is the date of the will.
- The solicitor must also attach a special certificate to the will, which can include details of where the will is to be kept.

Since this is a recent innovation, you should seek professional advice if you are considering this type of will. You can also get the relevant information from Her Majesty's Foreign Office or, if abroad, any British Embassy or Consulate.

ADDITIONAL DOCUMENTS

It may be that you want to include some other documents as part of your will. This is quite acceptable as long as:

- You make reference in your will to the documents involved.
- The documents can be clearly identified by such reference.
- Such documents actually exist at the time you make your will.

Provided these conditions are met, you do not have to go through the formality of having each one specially signed and witnessed.

AMENDMENTS

The best advice is to avoid making any amendments on your will. If you find there are mistakes or you have second thoughts about anything you have written, then you should scrap the whole will and start again.

If you do make any changes, these should be in ink. Alternatively, you could erase the relevant parts and either retype or stick a fresh piece of paper over the top with the revised copy.

In any event, all alterations must be signed or initialled by you and the two witnesses. And this must be done before you sign the will. Otherwise, the changes will not be valid.

There is a another device - known as a codicil - which can be used to add to or change parts of your will at a later date *(see Chapter 9)*. The formalities, however, can be complicated and it is best to avoid codicils altogether.

SIGNATURE

To be valid, a will must be signed by the person making it or, in exceptional circumstances, someone else present *(see page 52)*.

Use your usual full signature and preferably your proper name, although if you have another - such as a 'stage' or 'maiden' name - you can use this instead.

You can also 'sign' with a mark, for example a cross or even a thumb print, but not a seal. However, a rubber stamp containing your signature is acceptable.

Normally you should sign in front of at least two witnesses *(see overleaf)*, although you can do this beforehand as long as they verify your signature together.

Equally, the witnesses must sign the will in your presence, although it is not necessary for all of them to do this at the same time.

It is not essential to sign a will at the end, although this is the usual practice and does confirm your desire that everything in the will should be effective. It is also preferable, where the will is written on more than one page, to sign at the bottom of each. That would include the signature of witnesses, as well.

WITNESSES

As already mentioned, the signatures of at least two witnesses are needed to validate a will. Unless the person making the will is blind or illiterate, they do not need to know its contents. Essentially their function is to verify his or her signature.

It is usual, though not necessary, for the witnesses to sign below the signature of the person making the will. Equally, it is best to include a brief statement to the effect that they acknowledge that person's signature and were present together at the time. And they must add their address and occupation.

Apart from blind people, anyone can be a witness to a will, regardless of their background, occupation or social standing. It is advisable, however, to chose people whose credibility is not likely to be challenged. This will avoid any possible suggestion of improper practice, which could otherwise call into question the content or validity of the will.

You should remember that, where two witnesses are used, neither they nor their spouses are entitled to benefit from any part of your will or act as executors.

While it is necessary to have two witnesses unconnected with the terms of your will, should you for any reason decide to have more witnesses, then the others would be able to benefit, should you so desire. But this is an unnecessary complication.

One further point about witnesses. Any final judgement on the mental capacity of the person making the will is, of course, the responsibility of the courts. But where this could be called into question, one sensible precaution would be to include a doctor as one of the witnesses.

A FINAL GUIDE

Although it would be quite impossible here to offer anything but the minimum of suggestions as to how exactly you could write your will, since this must obviously depend on individual situations, the format below - as a standard solicitor's drawn form - includes the essential requirements to ensure your will is 'safe' and valid, where you wish to leave everything to your spouse or, in the event of her death, your children or other named beneficiaries.

This is the last Will and Testament of me

.... (full names)

of .... (full address)

in the County of ....

made this .... *day of* .... (full date)

one thousand nine hundred and ....

....

I, ... (full names)

hereby revoke all former testamentary
dispositions made by me and declare this
to be my last Will.

1. *I APPOINT my Wife/Husband*

.... (full names)

(hereinafter together called "my Trustees"
which expression where the context admits
includes any Trustee or Trustees hereof
for the time being whether original or
substituted) to be the Executors and
Trustees hereof and I declare that any
of my Trustees being a Solicitor or any
other person engaged in a profession or
business shall be entitled to charge and
be paid (without abatement) all usual
professional or other charges for business
done services rendered or time spent by
him or his firm in the administration of
my estate for the trusts hereof including
acts which a Trustee not engaged in any

profession or business could have done
personally.

2.   *I APPOINT* .... (full names)
.... *of* .... (full address)
....
to be the guardian after the death of my
Wife/Husband .... (full names)
of any of my children who may then be
minors.

3.   *IF my said Wife/Husband* .... (full names)
.... *aforesaid survives*
me by thirty days (but not otherwise)
I give to her/him absolutely (but subject
nevertheless to payment of my debts and
funeral and testamentary expenses) all my
estate both real and personal whatsoever
and wheresoever not hereby or by any
Codicil hereto otherwise specifically
disposed of.

4.   *IF my said Wife/Husband* .... (full names)
.... *aforesaid is not*
living at my death or does not survive me
by thirty days (but not otherwise) the
following provisions of this my Will
shall have effect.

5. *I GIVE all my estate both real
and personal whatsoever and wheresoever
not hereby or by any Codicil hereto
otherwise specifically disposed of unto
my Trustees UPON TRUST to raise and
discharge thereout my debts and funeral
and testamentary expenses and all
legacies given hereby or by any Codicil
hereto and any and all taxes payable by
reason of my death in respect of property
given free of tax and subject thereto
UPON TRUST to pay and divide the same
equally between such of my children*
.... (full names
of .... and addresses)
and ....
of..
*as shall survive me and attain the age of
eighteen years PROVIDED ALWAYS that if
any child of mine shall die in my
lifetime or before reaching the age of
eighteen years or marry under that age
such last mentioned child or children
shall take by substitution and if more
than one in equal shares the share of my
estate which his/her or their parent
would have taken if he or she had
survived me.*

6. *IF neither my Wife/Husband*

.... (full names)
nor my said children of any of their issue
are living at my death then I give all my
estate both real and personal whatsoever
and wheresoever unto my Trustees UPON
TRUST to raise and discharge thereout my
debts and funeral and testamentary
expenses and all legacies given hereby or
by any Codicil hereto and any and all
taxes payable by reason of my death in
respect of property given free of tax and
subject thereto UPON TRUST to pay
and divide the same equally between ...(full names
.... and addresses)
of..
and ....
of ....

7.   *MY Trustees shall have the*
following powers in addition to their
powers under the general law.

(a) *to apply for the benefit of any*
       beneficiary as my Trustees think
       fit the whole or any part of the
       income from that part of my estate
       to which he is entitled or may in
       future be entitled.

(b) *to apply for the benefit of any*

beneficiary as my Trustees think
fit the whole or any part of the
capital to which that beneficiary
is entitled or may in future be
entitled and on becoming absolutely
entitled he shall bring into account
any payments received under this
clause.

(c) to exercise the power of
appropriation conferred by S.41 of
the Administration of Estates Act
1925 without obtaining any of the
consents required by that section
and even though one or more of them
may be beneficially interested.

(d) to invest trust money and transpose
investment with the same full and
unrestricted freedom in their choice
of investments as if they were an
absolute beneficial owner and to
apply trust money at any time and
from time to time in the purchase
with vacant possession (upon trust
for sale with full power to postpone
sale) or in the improvement of any
freehold or leasehold house or
other dwelling and to permit the
same to be used as a residence by

any person or persons having an
interest or prospective interest in
my residuary estate upon such terms
and conditions from time to time as
my Trustees in their absolute
discretion may think fit.

(e) to insure against loss or damage by
fire or from any other risk any
property for the time being comprised
in my residuary estate to any amount
and even though a person is
absolutely entitled to the property
and to pay all premiums for any such
insurance at their discretion out of
the income or capital of my residuary
estate or the property itself and so
that any money received under such
insurance shall be applicable as if
it were proceeds of sale of the
property insured.

IN WITNESS whereof I have hereunto set my
hand this .... day of .... (full date)
one thousand nine hundred and ninety
....

SIGNED by the said .... (full names)
.... (signature)
in the presence of us both

who in his/her presence and   (signatures of
in the presence of each other   two witnesses
have hereunto signed our   + address
names as witnesses: and occupation)

(NOTE: No stamp or seal is required)

As already mentioned, you can purchase 'standard' will forms from any good stationers and there is a range that covers the majority of normal contingencies. If the example above does not meet your requirements, you should consider these as possible alternatives.

In any case, when in doubt you should seek professional advice or consult your Citizens' Advice Bureau.

I'M SURE HIS PEDIGREE IS EXCELLENT, BUT THE LAW STILL WON'T RECOGNISE YOUR POODLE AS A WITNESS.

What can I do about tax?

For a growing number of people, the question of tax and what effect this will have on their estate is one of the major considerations when making a will.

It goes without saying that the pattern and style of life has changed enormously over the last few decades. For example, a far larger proportion of the population owns a home, be it a house or flat, whose value has in some cases increased many times over.

One has only to look at the level of cover currently provided by insurance policies or the dramatic upward trend in the value of shares over the last few years.

The net result of these and other market factors is that the average person now faces the prospect of having tax deducted from at least part of his or her estate.

There are, of course, ways in which you can reduce or even eliminate the burden of tax and some of these are indicated below.

WARNING!

It cannot be stressed too strongly that the information given here must only be used as basic guidelines. It is not within the scope of this book to detail every relevant aspect of taxation and you should seek professional advice where this is likely to apply to your estate.

There are three Inland Revenue documents in particular that you will find very helpful. These are IHT3 (Introduction to inheritance tax), IR45 (What happens when someone dies) and IR65 (Giving to charity).

You may also wish to contact the Capital Taxes Office for clarification on certain points.

But first let us look at the tax itself and how it would normally apply in this situation.

INHERITANCE TAX

In simple terms, this is the tax levied on gifts from a person's estate over and above a certain threshold, which is subject to change, depending on the existing government's financial policy.

At present, this is linked to the retail price

index and increased accordingly each year. For 1993/4 the threshold - that is, the value of an estate above which tax may be payable - was £150,000 and the rate of tax was 40%.

For the purposes of tax, the value of the estate is that assessed immediately before the death of the person involved LESS any exemptions, which we will be looking at shortly.

That in itself may sound reasonably straightforward. But there is, however, a further significant condition concerning tax liability.

Taking into account the various exemptions, inheritance tax can also be levied on gifts and transfers made within a period of seven years preceding a person's death.

The question, therefore, of how much tax might have to be paid on your estate when you die will basically depend on the following:

- The assessed value of your estate.
- What you gave in the way of gifts in the seven years prior to your death.
- What gifts, if any, in your estate are subject to exemption under current conditions.

EXEMPT GIFTS

Although the examples quoted here are by no means exhaustive, they should give you a reasonable idea of what you can give away within seven years of your death without incurring any tax liability.

Incidentally, it follows that any gift made more than seven years before your death is free of tax, regardless of its size or to whom it was given.

Do bear in mind, however, that as with all aspects of this book that are subject to legislation, the information given is current but could change at any time.

Items exempt from inheritance tax include:

TO INDIVIDUALS

- Any gift to your spouse UNLESS he or she is resident abroad, in which case the limit is £55,000.
- The full estate of armed service personnel who die as a result of a wound, accident or disease while on 'active duty' under warlike conditions.
- Gifts regarded as items of normal expenditure from your income before your death, which are not considered to have altered your standard of living.
- Gifts to one or more people up to combined total of £3000 during any one tax year AND individual gifts of up to £250 each to an unlimited number of people provided, within this category, no-one receives more than £250 in any one tax year. This means the same person cannot benefit from both gifts.
- Wedding gifts to your children up to £5000, to your grandchildren or remoter relatives up to

£2500 and to others up to £1000.

- Maintenance gifts to your spouse or former spouse, your children or dependent relatives. 'Children' here include adopted, illegitimate and stepchildren up to the age of eighteen or the end of full-time education, whichever is later. 'Dependent relatives' include the aged or infirm who require help and widowed parents who cannot support themselves.

TO GROUPS

- Gifts to charity
- Gifts to institutions concerned with national heritage including most museums and art galleries. (You should seek advice here as to what exactly qualifies.)
- Gifts to political parties, though there is a limit of £100,000 if made within a year of your death.

EXEMPT PROPERTY

The laws relating to tax relief on certain gifts of business property or holdings, such as shares, has recently been changed and in some cases, for example, this relief can be up to 100%.

It is potentially a critical area, especially for small private companies and partnerships and sole proprietors, where unexpectedly high tax liability could threaten the future existence of the business.

If you are in such a situation, you MUST

seek professional advice on the possibilities of tax exemption.

POTENTIAL LIABILITY

Any gift made within seven years of your death that does not fall within one of the 'exemption' categories will automatically be included in the value of your estate and therefore become liable for tax.

Where applicable, the actual percentage of the gift on which inheritance tax is due and the rate at which it is payable will depend on exactly when the gift was made - that is, the number of years before your death - based on the following scale:

- 6-7 years - 20% of gift at rate of 8%
- 5-6 years - 40% of gift at rate of 16%
- 4-5 years - 60% of gift at rate of 24%
- 3-4 years - 80% of gift at rate of 32%
- Up to 3 years - 100% of gift at rate of 40%

From this, you can see that there is still some advantage to be gained from making gifts, providing it is done at least three years before your death.

There can, however, still be a problem even here if you continue to benefit from something you have given as a gift. One obvious example would be a house, which you officially transferred perhaps to one of your children. If you continued to live there until you died - or even moved out to live permanently elsewhere within the all-important seven-year period - for tax purposes the value of the house would have to be included in your estate.

DEED OF VARIATION

This is a device with which beneficiaries can, within a two-year period following your death, alter the provision you made for them, even if they have already received the gift. The same applies under the rules of intestacy.

Under this deed, they can redirect, give or disclaim the gift. The significance of this is that tax is then only payable under the conditions of the new provision.

So, for example, one of your children can make a deed of variation for a gift on which he or she was due to pay inheritance tax in favour of your spouse, which would remove the liability.

A deed of variation must be put in writing, make specific reference to the relevant provision in the will, carry the signature of the beneficiary concerned and sent to the Capital Taxes Office.

However, should such an action increase the tax liability elsewhere, the executors must be party to the deed and are entitled to refuse if there are insufficient funds in the estate to pay the increase.

WHO PAYS THE TAX?

This is not always as straightforward as it might seem, since there can be several variables. In principle, however, the matter of responsibility depends on what, if any, provisions exist within the will for the payment of tax and whether gifts were made in the will or before the person's death.

MAKING PROVISION

Where it is clear that your estate exceeds the threshold and tax will be payable, you should certainly make provision for this in your will. It is essentially a question of commonsense.

To avoid the need to sell property, which you want the relevant beneficiary to keep, you must make sure that you leave enough of pecuniary value available to meet the necessary liability. Otherwise some would-be beneficiaries could end up at best disappointed and at worst with nothing.

Where you have not provided for the payment of tax, this is taken from the residue, wherever and however that is available. And the liability for such payments rests with those responsible for the administration of your estate, whether or not a will exists.

INSURE AGAINST TAX

One useful way of providing for possible tax liability is through life insurance policies.

Where these are in your name and for your benefit, then their value is added to that of your estate. But if you make a gift of the policy to someone else before you die, then it is only the premium payment - and not the value - that is liable to tax, should this be within seven years of your death.

Better still, if you take out the policy for the benefit of a member of your family, the full maturity value payable on your death will go to them and therefore will not become part of your estate.

Such money could then be used to help pay off any tax or could solve a cash problem for a surviving relative, particularly your spouse.

GIFTS IN THE WILL

Where you leave money as a gift to someone in your will and there is a tax liability involved, you can stipulate who in effect pays it.

Bear in mind here that, in the absence of any instruction, tax will be taken from the residue - and thus reduce its value for that particular beneficiary.

You can either make the gift 'free of tax', which means payment from the residue, or 'subject to tax', which means payment is taken from that particular gift - that is, from its beneficiary.

GIFTS OUTSIDE THE WILL

Where you make non-exempted gifts within seven years of your death and your estate becomes liable for tax, then the responsibility for payment of the tax due on those gifts rests primarily with their recipients.

If, twelve months after your death, this remains unpaid, then your 'personal representatives', which normally means the executors, are also liable.

The implications of such a situation can be embarrassing to all parties concerned and it is therefore most advisable to think carefully before making such gifts - and to warn those receiving them of the possible repercussions.

HOW IS THE TAX PAYABLE?

In most cases, any tax liability is deducted from the value of your estate before the relevant gifts are made to beneficiaries, although this of course depends on the exact terms of your will, as has already been highlighted.

It is then the responsibility of those administering your estate to forward the required amount to the Inland Revenue once probate - or official approval - has been granted over the terms, value and intended relevant distribution of assets.

It is quite possible that, at the time tax is payable, the value of the estate is still an estimated, rather than actual, figure. This is often the case where property is waiting to be sold and a sale may only be secured many months later. Should the price achieved be less than the initial valuation, an adjustment to the tax paid will be made and the estate refunded accordingly with interest.

There are instances where some tax liabilities can be paid in instalments, usually involving equal amounts over ten years.

Examples include buildings, land and certain types of shares and securities where it can be shown that to pay off the tax in one sum would result in real hardship.

This system is useful since those beneficiaries involved can avoid the need to sell off property left to them in order to meet the tax liability, even though it can mean paying interest on the instalments.

For further information on this method of payment, you should seek professional advice or contact the Capital Taxes Office.

REMEMBER YOUR WILL

The economic climate is subject to both dramatic and sometimes imperceptible changes. Often one is swept along with the general tide or, conversely, remains oblivious of subtle alterations in circumstance.

One of the obvious dangers you must remain constantly aware of is how such fluctuations, both up and down, can effect the provisions of your last or existing will.

No-one is suggesting that every market surge - or collapse - should send you rushing to write a new one. But it is important that you consider the implications of such variations and regularly review your own personal situation.

The ideal, perhaps, is to make provisions that cater for the unexpected so that you need to rewrite your will as infrequently as possible.

CHAPTER 8

What do I do with my will?

O nce you have written your will, signed and had this witnessed, put the document into a secure envelope and write clearly on the front: "The Last Will and Testament of ....".

The real significance of a will is that it reflects exactly how you want your estate to be disposed of after your death. The tragedy would be that, if it could not be found and therefore presumed destroyed, your wishes would not be carried out.

It therefore goes without saying that you need to keep it somewhere safe BUT also in a place where it can be easily retrieved - either by you, should you decide to rewrite it, or by those responsible for its administration when you die.

It is not the intention of this book to advise you as to the safest or most sensible place to keep your will. The following are merely helpful suggestions.

YOUR BANK

This is probably the most obvious place and also one of the most accessible. It is also very secure, since no-one bar yourself will be able to gain access to it until after your death.

YOUR SOLICITOR

This practice is probably most common where you have a firm of solicitors which has been looking after your - and your family's - affairs for a considerable length of time. You are known personally and quite possibly your own solicitor is fully conversant with the terms of your will.

Under their code of practice, solicitors are not allowed to divulge personal information to third parties, in which case you should be assured of adequate security here, as well.

RECORDS OFFICE

You can, if you wish, deposit your will with the Record Keeper at Somerset House in London or, in the case of Northern Ireland, with the Master of the Probate and Matrimonial Office at the Royal Courts of Justice in Belfast.

A small fee is payable for this service and you will receive a special envelope in which to put your will.

On receipt of the will, you will be given a certificate of deposit, which you have to produce to gain access to your will. The same applies for your executors, so they must be told where you keep your certificate.

Naturally, unauthorized access to this document is impossible.

For more information, you should contact the relevant office:

- Somerset House - 071-936 7000
- Royal Courts of Justice - 0232 235111

PERSONAL RECORD

Before you deposit your will in a secure place, take a photocopy and keep this somewhere safe at home. It will then be handy for future reference, particularly if you decide at any time you need to change any of the provisions it contains. You will, of course, need to substitute and destroy the original if this happens.

And don't forget to tell your family and executors where you have put both your original will and the copy.

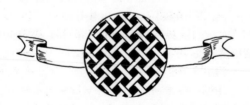

CHAPTER 9

Can I change my will?

Y ou can change a will whenever you want and as many times as you want. In principle, it is always your last will which is valid and, by implication, any previous ones become invalid.

It is, however, a wise precaution to destroy any previous wills, either by tearing them up or burning them. Just crossing them out is not sufficient.

You can also invalidate a will by removing your signature - or, equally, those of the witnesses - from it.

If, for any reason, you destroy only part of the will, what remains will still be valid, provided that this still meets the necessary minimum requirements, such as signature and witnesses.

Should you have included codicils *(see page 97)* as part of your will, these must also be destroyed. Otherwise, they could remain valid even if you write a new will.

DESTROYING A WILL

Although the net result of tearing up or burning a will is its physical destruction, the law states that such an act must be intended - that is, not accidental.

This, of course, is not always that easy to prove. And the situation is further complicated by the fact that there can be no obvious presumption that you have destroyed your will just because it cannot be found after your death.

In case of accidental loss or destruction, a copy of a will is normally accepted as evidence of the 'existence' of an original.

To safeguard against possible confusion, the following procedures should be followed:

- *Burn your previous will.*
- *Burn any copies of that will.*
- *Put your new will in safe-keeping.*
- *Keep a copy of your new will.*

The two main reasons for writing a new will are a change of mind or a change of circumstance - or both.

CHANGE OF MIND

It is quite possible - and permissible - to change your mind over specific bequests for whatever reason.

Perhaps you have made provisions in your will to ensure the financial security or welfare of your children. Over a period of time it becomes evident that one child will be more in need of such help than another and you decide to alter the relevant gifts accordingly.

Possibly you may have nominated a particular charity as a beneficiary, but later feel that another cause is more deserving.

A situation might even arise where you had previously wanted to leave something to a good friend but you have since fallen out and decide that such a gift would no longer be appropriate.

It is, of course, impossible to list all the likely reasons for wanting to change your will under such circumstances. Suffice it to say that you are free to rewrite your will when you want.

CHANGE OF CIRCUMSTANCE

The younger you are when you first make a will, the greater the likelihood that you will need to change this as your personal and financial situations change.

The most usual circumstances are those under which you should make a will in the first place. These have already been discussed earlier in the book *(see Chapter 3)*.

However, there are three in particular that deserve further qualification here - marriage, divorce and death.

MARRIAGE

When you get married, generally speaking any will you have made previously becomes invalid and you need to write a new one. This does not apply, however, in Scotland *(see Appendix II)*.

There is an important qualification to make here.

An existing will can remain valid if, within its terms, it is obvious that you are intending to get married and to whom and that it is your wish for the existing will to remain operative.

If this is the case, you should also have made clear whether you want all or just some of the provisions to remain intact.

You may feel this is unnecessarily complicated and the simplest and most satisfactory solution would be to rewrite your will.

DIVORCE

As has already been mentioned *(see Chapter 3)*, the effect of a divorce is to invalidate any mention of or benefit to a former spouse within the terms of an existing will - unless you have made specific provision to the contrary.

If you therefore decide, after divorcing your

spouse, that you would still like to leave him or her something when you die, you must make a new will to include the necessary provision.

If you don't, then the original bequest to your spouse (as was) will go directly to your children (if, of course, you have any) and your former spouse gets nothing.

It should be stressed here that only those clauses in your will referring to your former spouse become invalid. The rest of your will would remain effective.

DEATH

The situation might well arise that an original beneficiary of your will dies. Where you have already made provision for this, there would be no need to change the will.

However, you should bear in mind what could happen with the gift should no provision exist and, depending on the circumstances, make the necessary changes to give that gift to someone else of your choice.

WRITING A CODICIL

This is the term used for a supplement to a will, where the testator has decided to add or alter something after completing the original document.

Codicils should be presented on separate sheets of paper and are subject to similar conditions as the will itself - for example, those involving signing and witnessing.

Although, properly drafted, they carry the same validity, there can be complications. They are therefore not to be recommended.

Not for the first time in this book, it must be said that if you want to make any changes in your will, rewrite it completely and destroy the old one.

CHAPTER 10

Can my will be changed?

The underlying principle of making a will is that it enables you to choose, subject to any tax considerations, where exactly you want your estate to go.

However, there are certain conditions under which a court can agree to changes in your will or, indeed, authorize them itself for various reasons.

The most obvious is where errors or ambiguities exist in any of the provisions made in the will. But there are other principles on which courts have considerable powers to act, particularly those of unfairness or those of unreasonable conditions - or 'contrary to public policy'.

It is worth repeating here that if it can be proved that you were, through mental illness, incapable of rational judgement at the time you made your will, a court can act accordingly and authorize what changes it deems necessary.

Although it would, of course, be impossible

to list every relevant situation, the following examples should give you some guidance as to the potential pitfalls.

RECTIFYING A WILL

Where there are clearly seen to be mistakes in the actual wording of a will or it is worded in such a way as to make the instructions or meaning ambiguous, a court can make the necessary changes. This is known as rectifying a will.

However, any such alterations must reflect or concur with the overall intentions of the testator and the court will assess this on the basis of any other available evidence. This could include an earlier verbal intention or relevant correspondence, for example.

Any beneficiary under the will can apply to the court to effect such changes, although this must normally be within six months of probate. After this period, the administrators of the estate are not responsible for any bequest already distributed which turns out to be contrary to a part of the will that has been rectified.

Those who have already received such a bequest might, however, face problems since the court can order that gift to be handed back.

CLAIMING FROM A WILL

The idea that you can leave your property, possessions and money to whoever or whatever you like remains true - to a point. And that point concerns not those you wish to benefit but those you don't - or, more tactfully, those you have chosen to exclude from your bequests.

Most recently under the Inheritance (Provision for Family and Dependants) Act of 1975, it is possible for certain specified people, who are not already provided for, to claim money from your estate through the courts.

In fact, this applies whether or not you have made a will - and only affects wills made in England and Wales.

Those entitled to claim include:

- Your spouse
- A former spouse who has not remarried
- Your children
- Any stepchildren by your last or previous marriages
- Anyone you partly or fully maintained prior to your death

SPOUSE

Your spouse can claim on your estate even if he or she remarries after your death. And a court has the power to give any amount it decides is reasonable, even if there is evidence that the money is not required for maintenance - that is, everyday living expenses. However, any regular payments would cease when that person remarried or died.

FORMER SPOUSE

The sole condition under which former spouses can claim is that they have not remarried. And any such claim could normally only be for necessary maintenance, which would cease if they remarried. There is one exception. If your death occurs within a year of divorce or legal separation, your former spouse can make a full claim.

CHILDREN

Here again, any claim by your children could only be on the basis of hardship - that is, essential maintenance.

STEPCHILDREN

This includes anyone you treated as your own child and supported, even if they were the offspring of a spouse by different marriages, as well as those who are illegitimate or those conceived before, but not born till after, your death.

Their claim, too, can only cover maintenance.

DEPENDANTS

This necessarily covers a much wider range of potential claimants. And, again, only maintenance is applicable here.

There has to be evidence that you were partly or fully maintaining that person prior to your death. Such support does not have to be financial, however. You could have been providing accommodation and food, for example, whether or not there was a contribution from the person involved. Obvious examples of those entitled to claim would include someone with whom you were cohabiting, but not married to, or an ageing, dependent relative living under your roof.

AND THIS IS....

WARNING!

If you try and beat the system by giving away money or property before you die in order to avoid the possibility of it passing to people you do not want to benefit, you could be creating major problems for the original beneficiaries.

If a court decides that any gifts made within six years of your death were done so with this objective in mind, then it has the power to order such gifts to be handed back and redistributed to meet existing claims.

As you can see, this could cause acute embarrassment to those who received your gifts in all innocence. It should, however, be stressed that it is up to the court to decide what order, if any, it makes in such a situation.

One further word of warning. Where any claim on your estate is upheld, existing beneficiaries could get less than you had intended.

This will, of course, depend on the final ruling, but the court has the powers to take whatever money is needed to meet the claims from any part of your estate.

INSOLVENCY

Anyone considering a claim under the conditions already mentioned should, however, remember that there has to be something in the estate to claim against.

No-one can make a claim on an estate that is insolvent - that is, where the debts are larger than the assets.

CHANGING CONDITIONS

You have already seen how a court can rectify any part of your will that contains obvious errors or ambiguities and can rule in favour of certain claimants you have excluded in your bequests.

There is, however, another situation in which a court has the power to intervene and, where it judges appropriate, possibly to rule against any of your specific intentions.

This relates directly to any conditions you may have imposed on a beneficiary in order to receive a gift which are considered unreasonable - or 'contrary to public policy'.

If the court decides this is the case, that particular condition attached to the gift becomes void and does not have to be fulfilled.

So what happens to that gift?

This will depend on the condition attached, as follows:

- IF the condition involved something being done

before the beneficiary could have the gift,
THEN the beneficiary does not receive the gift.

- IF the condition involved something being done
  after the beneficiary received the gift,
  THEN the beneficiary can have the gift without
  the condition, of course.

If the beneficiary does not receive the gift,
then who does? This will depend on what other
provisions, if any, exist, as follows:

- IF provision has been made for that gift to go to
  another person in the event that the intended
  person does not receive it,
  THEN the beneficiary named in the provision
  gets the gift.

- IF no such provision has been made,
  THEN the gift becomes part of the residue of
  the estate.

It is clear from the above that the potential
problems surrounding conditions that could be
regarded as unreasonable should deter you from
including ANY conditions, unless you feel they are
absolutely necessary.

It would be impossible to list everything that
might be judged 'unreasonable'. But the following
should provide you with at least some guidelines as

to what would or would not be acceptable.

INCENTIVE TO BREAK UP A MARRIAGE

Any condition that provided an incentive to end a marriage would be void. And this could also be the case even if it was not your intention that this should be the result.

INCENTIVE TO REMAIN CELIBATE

To make a gift on the condition that the beneficiary NEVER got married would be considered unreasonable. However, if you state that marriage could not be with a particular person or someone from a particular group, this could be valid. Incidentally, there is nothing to stop you providing for people UNTIL they marry or even specifying a minimum age for marriage.

INCENTIVE NOT TO REMARRY

It is perfectly legitimate for you to make a bequest to your spouse on the basis that he or she does not remarry. You cannot, however, make the same condition for any other beneficiary.

SEPARATING CHILDREN

Any condition that involved children being separated from their parents would not be acceptable. This does not necessarily apply, however, to adult children - only dependent ones.

RELIGIOUS PRACTICE

This is not an easy area, since it can often be open to interpretation and, in that event, a court would normally judge the condition void. This would include such expressions as 'practising a religion'. Specific conditions such as becoming or ceasing to be a member of a particular religion could, however, be considered 'reasonable'.

GENERAL BEHAVIOUR

Although it would be impossible to define this exactly, conditions relating to behaviour are often accepted. This is also true where a beneficiary has to obey the wishes of a specified person or satisfy the executors of his or her behaviour.

CRIME

You cannot make any gift conditional on the beneficiary performing an act that is against the law.

OPEN TO INTERPRETATION

As already mentioned, any condition that is open to different interpretations will inevitably be considered invalid. This is not necessarily because your intention was unreasonable, but simply because it was not clear.

ENFORCING CONDITIONS

It is one thing to make a condition and another to enforce it. But the courts are empowered to ensure that any acceptable conditions are met. If they find this is not the case, they can take away the relevant gift.

LOSING THE RIGHT

Apart from a failure to meet any conditions attached to a gift, there are other circumstances under which beneficiaries can forfeit the right to a bequest.

The most dramatic example would be where a beneficiary was convicted of the murder of the testator or was an accomplice to the act. In such an event, the person could not receive anything under the will. This does not necessarily apply, however, in a case of manslaughter.

A court can also stop anyone from receiving a bequest where there is evidence of coercion, excessive badgering, unreasonable influence or fraud - where, for example, a lie has been told in order to influence the testator to make a particular gift.

Probate and how it works

In simple terms, probate is official confirmation of executors' powers to administer the estate of a dead person. This is evidenced by a document known as a 'grant of representation', which enables those dealing with a will to gain access to relevant financial information or essential documents.

Anyone charged with the administration of an estate has, of course, automatic authority to act immediately following the death of the testator. But, as you will see, there are certain areas where evidence of probate will be required.

If no will exists or no executors have been appointed, then it is necessary to get 'letters of administration', which involves a similar procedure.

WHY PROBATE?

Under common law, probate has basically three objectives. These are:

- To safeguard creditors of the deceased.
- To ensure reasonable provision is made for the deceased's dependants.
- To distribute the balance of the estate in accordance with the known or presumed intentions of the deceased.

Whether or not probate is necessary depends mainly on the amount of money involved. Where the sums are small, the financial institutions concerned will normally not require to see the grant of representation. But bear in mind, however, that no-one is obliged to release money without this document - or letters of administration.

To give you some idea, such bodies as the post office, bank, building society, Department of National Savings or insurance company will usually be helpful where the situation is straightforward and the money involved not too great and will make the necessary payments without evidence of probate.

However, where large sums of money, stocks and shares and property sale or transfer are concerned, the institutions involved will almost certainly want to see the grant of probate or letters of administration before releasing what they hold on behalf of the deceased.

Those responsible for administering the estate must find out from the bodies concerned what the procedure is.

WHO APPLIES FOR PROBATE?

Where a will exists and executors have been appointed...

THEN any one of them can make the application.

Where a will exists but no executors have been appointed...

THEN the person who benefits from the whole estate - or the residue left after all the other bequests have been met - should make the application. This would equally be the case where any named executor, for whatever reason, cannot or does not want to do so.

Where no will exists...

THEN the next of kin can apply for probate in the following order of preference:

• The surviving spouse
• A child of the deceased
• A parent of the deceased
• A brother or sister of the deceased
• Another relative of the deceased

There are a few points to be made about the above list. For example, the person applying for probate must be over eighteen. The term 'child' includes any that are illegitimate. And if a child dies before the deceased, then one of his or her children (ie the grandchildren) can apply for probate.

APPLYING FOR PROBATE

This can be done through any Probate Registry or Probate Office. Normally there is one in every main town. As a matter of convenience, you can choose the nearest and not necessarily one in the area where the deceased lived.

There is an important administrative point to make here. If you are writing, then you should always address your correspondence to a registry - and not an office.

Alternatively, you can contact the Probate Personal Application Department at Somerset House in London (Tel: 071-936 6983).

WHAT TO DO NEXT

There are, of course, a number of things that must now be done, depending on what the deceased person has left in the way of property, money, savings, investments and insurance.

DEATH CERTIFICATE

Obtaining a death certificate is, naturally enough, essential since a copy of this will have to be included with every letter written to the relevant bodies or institutions. This is provided when a death is registered, as required by law, with the local Registrar of Births and Deaths.

THE WILL

Hopefully there is no problem in tracing the whereabouts of the dead person's will *(see Chapter 8)*. Either the next of kin or one of the executors (if that is not the same person) should do this and at least one copy should be made and kept by an executor, just in case the original gets lost.

THE ESTATE

This is probably the most onerous part of the executors' duties, since it is necessary to list everything that the deceased owned or held in the way of property, capital, assets and personal possessions. Against these, a value must be added. A reasonable estimate of such things as furniture, household items, clothes and general personal possessions is usually acceptable and certainly it is helpful if previous valuations for insurance purposes are available *(see Appendix IV)* for this purpose.

For the rest, a precise value must be sought and it is principally for these items that a grant of probate is often essential.

What exactly this includes will depend on individual circumstances. But some of the more obvious areas would be:

- **PROPERTY**
  Whatever value is put on on a house or flat, the Inland Revenue can always insist on its own valuation. Therefore it is unwise to make a personal judgement here and preferable to have the property valued professionally. There may still be a mortgage on the property, in which case one will need to know the amount outstanding. This will require a letter to the mortgagee from the executor with the name of the deceased and the exact date of death.

- **CAPITAL**
  Here the executor will have to write to any bank, building society or post office where the deceased held accounts to find out how much money exists in each. Again the name of the deceased and date of death will be required. In the case of the bank, the executor should also ask for any other relevant details, such as any important documents, share certificates or valuables that the bank might be holding on behalf of the deceased. With stocks and shares, the bank will normally ascertain the value for the executor. Otherwise it will be necessary to write to the broker or individual companies concerned.

- **SAVINGS**
  Where this involves insurance policies, a letter

should be sent to the relevant companies, with the same details, asking for clarification of the amounts payable under each policy. With premium bonds, one should write to the Bond & Stock Office at Lytham St Annes in Lancashire. These can be cashed in once probate is granted or can be left as an investment for up to twelve months after the date of death. As far as savings certificates are concerned, the place to write to is the Savings Certificate Office in Durham. The information required would be a list of certificates, when they were bought and their current value.

- **PENSIONS**
  Full details of any pension funds should be obtained from the appropriate employers or institutions, again by letter with the full name of the deceased and date of death.

HANDY FORM

Where savings exist with a government - rather than private - institution, there is a helpful form which an executor can use to obtain the necessary information and payment. This is the SB4, available from most post offices.

- **MONEY OWING**

  If there is evidence of any money owing to the deceased, this should also be noted and every effort made to recover such amounts. Legal advice and help may be required here. The executor should also bear in mind that there could be refunds for certain items paid in advance. Car insurance, rates and certain charges are just a few examples. A standard letter should be written to those concerned.

- **MONEY OWED**

  It is very important to make a list of any amounts owed by the deceased at the time of death, since these would have to be paid out of the estate. Obvious items include outstanding bills, rates, hire purchase arrangements and bank overdrafts. One essential area to check is that of tax. A letter must be sent to the local tax office to see whether there is any outstanding liability on behalf of the deceased OR, equally importantly, whether any tax refund is due. If it is not clear as to exactly who all the creditors are, then the executor should put advertisements to that effect in the London Gazette and one newspaper local to the area in which the deceased lived. Here a deadline must be given for creditors to submit any claim. This must be a minimum of two months.

  It is also the responsibility of an executor to

notify the current situation to any creditor of whom he or she is aware.

- **EXPENSES**
  A full account must be obtained from the funeral company once the ceremony has been held. Equally, it is necessary to make sure note has been taken of any provisions in the will for the use of professional services and the charges connected with them. These would normally have been agreed in advance.

LEGAL ADVICE

Although probate is not necessarily a complicated procedure, the reality will depend on the nature of individual estates.

Where these include large sums of money or involved property settlements - or, for example, one has to trace beneficiaries whose whereabouts are not known - then it is definitely advisable to seek professional help.

And this would also apply where an executor is in any doubt as to what he or she has to do. With the level of responsibility attached to such a task, mistakes can prove very costly.

THE FINAL STAGES

Before probate is finally granted, there are certain procedures which have to be followed. They should normally be just a formality, but they are necessary all the same.

Apart from sending the death certificate and the original of the will (not a copy) to the Probate Registry, the executor also needs to complete a series of forms, which are obtainable from the registry or a Probate Office.

Then the executor will be required to attend an interview at an office of his or her choice to complete the formalities.

The forms mentioned above include:

- PROBATE APPLICATION FORM - PR 83
  This involves filling in details of the deceased, relatives of the deceased, the will and the executors. Here he or she must indicate the preferred location for the interview.

- RETURN OF THE WHOLE ESTATE - CAP 44
  This requires some care when completing, since it concerns specific information about the estate of the deceased. It also includes a declaration at the end for the executor to sign.

- INLAND REVENUE CAPITAL TAXES OFFICE - CAP 37
  This is concerned uniquely with property, be it land or buildings, owned by the deceased and is

for the purposes of inheritance tax. Details of
any property need to be completed here.

- INLAND REVENUE CAPITAL TAXES OFFICE - CAP 40
  This requires information on all the deceased's
  stocks, shares and securities, with valuations.
  There is a useful free booklet to help with this
  form, which is obtainable from the Capital
  Taxes Office (Tel: 071-603 4622).

THE INTERVIEW

This will be held according to any specific
instructions given by the executor with regard to
location and time.

As far as all the documentation is
concerned, this can either be sent or delivered in
advance or produced at the time of the interview -
by prior arrangement with the relevant Probate
Registry or Office.

If the application is a personal, rather than
professional one, the individual concerned should
have no fears about the nature of the interview. It
is not an inquisition, but simply a means of sorting
out any possible problems.

If there are problems arising from any of the
documents and these cannot be solved on the spot,
it may be necessary to convene a further interview.
This could happen where certain clarification is
required from a third party.

The most important forms are those relating

to inheritance tax, since probate cannot be granted until this is paid - either in full or, at least, the first instalment *(see Chapter 7)*.

At the end of the session, the executor will be required to confirm in front of the probate officer that the information given in the various forms is true to the best of his or her knowledge.

There is a probate fee to be paid, of which the executor needs to be aware. But, even with larger estates, this would only be in the region of several hundred pounds. Where the documents have been received in advance, a estimate would be sent to the executor. In any event, a scale of fees is available from any probate office.

PAYING TAX

There is a time limit of six months in which any tax due should be paid, whether in full or by instalments *(see Chapter 7)*.

The Probate Registry will inform the executor or personal representative, where an individual application for probate is being made, of the exact tax liability and where he or she should send the necessary payment.

There are some alternative methods by which inheritance tax can be paid. These include the direct transfer of National Savings and certain types of property and possession that are judged to be of historic interest.

The Capital Taxes Office will supply the

relevant information on such procedures.

OPENING AN ACCOUNT

It must have become evident by now that the various financial obligations of an executor often require the need to have ready access to funds to make certain payments and, indeed, to arrange for the temporary deposit of assets prior to their distribution to the individual beneficiaries.

Where the bequest of the deceased is simple - that is, leaving everything to the spouse - and the bank account is in joint names, then the problem may not arise.

In any other situation, the executors should open a special bank account through which they can receive and pay out money as required, whether for tax or other purposes.

And where there is likely to be some delay in the granting of probate, an investment account could well enable the estate to benefit. However, it must be pointed out that the interest on such an account could be liable to tax, depending on the total valuation of the estate.

GRANTING PROBATE

After a minimum period of delay, normally a few weeks, a grant of probate will be sent to the executors. This document will give final authority for the administration of the estate of the deceased.

This is important, since it allows the executors to gain the release of all money (or certificates, where applicable) held by the various institutions to distribute according to the terms of the will.

For a small fee, copies of this grant can be obtained and will normally be required to secure the necessary release of assets held by the different institutions.

In the case of a personal representative, this will not be a grant of probate but letters of administration. The authority, however, is the same.

Making a will in Scotland

Much of what has been covered in this book as regards making a will applies throughout the United Kingdom. However, there are some differences for a will made in Scotland, which are highlighted below.

If you are in any doubt, of course, you should contact a solicitor who knows the law in relation to wills.

- INTESTACY
  If you do not make a will in Scotland before you die, the consequences are different from the rest of the United Kingdom *(see Chapter 2)* as follows:

IF	there is a spouse
BUT	no other close family, such as children, parents, brothers or sisters,
THEN	the spouse benefits from the whole estate.

IF   there is a spouse
AND   there are children,
THEN the spouse can have your property (or
        £50,000 if it is worth more), furniture
        and personal possessions up to a value
        of £10,000, cash up to £15,000 and a
        third of the remainder of the estate
        (excluding other property)
AND   the children (or their children) share
        what is left in equal proportions.

IF   there is no spouse
BUT   there are children,
THEN they (including illegitimate and adopted
        but NOT stepchildren) or their children
        benefit from the estate in equal shares.

IF   there is no spouse or children
BUT   there are parents, brothers and sisters,
THEN the parents take half the estate and the
        other half is divided equally between any
        brothers and sisters (or their children)
OR   where only one of these groups are alive,
        those concerned benefit from the whole
        estate.

IF   none of the above is applicable,
THEN the following benefit in order:

•   Full uncles/aunts (or their children)

- Half uncles/aunts (or their children)
- Grandparents
- Full great uncles/aunts (or descendants)
- Half great uncles/aunts (or descendants)
- Great grandparents

IF   no relatives can be traced,
THEN the Crown takes the estate and can
         distribute it among anyone with a
         reasonable claim, such as a close
         relationship with the deceased.

- AGE

Whereas in the rest of the United Kingdom you
normally have to be over eighteen to make a
will (*see Chapter 1*), in Scotland the age limit is
lower. For a male it is over fourteen and over
twelve for a female.

- MARRIAGE

Unlike in the rest of the United Kingdom,
marriage does not revoke an existing will.

- CHILDREN

Whereas in the rest of the United Kingdon this
applies to illegitimate and adopted children, in
Scotland you have to specify their status in the
will. Another important difference is that if you
have children after making a will and have not
made any mention of them, then the will is

considered void. In such a situation, you must make a new will.

• PROPERTY

Where you own property in both Scotland and other parts of the United Kingdon - and the Republic of Ireland, for that matter - these can be dealt with together using the same trustees.

• PRESENTATION

If you write the whole of your will by hand, then you do not need any witnesses. You must sign at the bottom of every page - not just the last one. And if the will is not completely hand-written, then you will need two witnesses, who must also sign at the bottom of each page, as well as at the end.

• CLAIMS

In Scotland your spouse and children have more rights to claim against the estate than in the rest of the United Kingdom, even if it is your expressed intention to exclude them.

Equally, the law works against any claims from others who were partly or totally dependent on you before your death.
For example,

IF   there is a spouse
BUT   there are no children,

THEN the spouse can claim half of the estate (excluding property).

IF   there is a spouse
AND there are children,
THEN the spouse and children can each claim a third of the estate (excluding property).

IF   there is no spouse
BUT there are children,
THEN the children can claim one half of the estate (excluding property).

It is, of course, up to those concerned to decide whether they will benefit more from accepting the existing terms of the will or by making a claim against them. But they can only do one or the other - not both.

As with all the information given in this book, where there is any element of doubt or you need further clarification or explanation, you should seek professional advice or contact a Citizens' Advice Bureau or the DSS.

A seviceman's will

As has already been mentioned *(see Chapter 1)*, the minimum age limit for making a will does not apply to members of the armed forces on active military service, who can do so whatever their age.

It is important to note here that the special laws relating to servicemen and women only apply in relation to operational conditions - that is, in a war situation. They do not apply just because a person happens to be a soldier, sailor or airman. The key phrase is 'active military service'.

MAKING THE WILL

The will itself can either be written down or the intentions of the person making it passed on verbally to a witness. Here, again, the law is different. Unlike with a normal will, the witness can be a beneficiary and receive gifts from the estate.

In the case of a written will, this can even be

in pencil and does not have to be witnessed. Equally, a single witness is acceptable.

If the person involved gives verbal instructions as to how he or she wants the estate to be disposed of, all that is required is a clear intention that such instructions should be carried out if and when the situation arises.

There can, of course, be problems with an informal will of this kind and certainly anyone serving in the armed forces would be wise to make a formal will under the normal conditions.

REVOKING A WILL

Whether a will was made in writing or verbally, it can be revoked at any time by similar means - that is, in writing or by word of mouth.

But this only appiies while that person remains in the armed forces. If he or she leaves to become a civilian, then a new will under normal conditions will have to be made.

Equally, a minor returning to civilian life cannot revoke his or her will until the age of eighteen.

DYING ON ACTIVE SERVICE

Where a person dies on active military service, there is no inheritance tax liability on his or her estate.

Making life easier for others

One of the greatest frustrations for those involved in administering an estate - and, equally, those hoping to benefit from it - comes when they cannot lay their hands on all the necessary documentation or paperwork.

Not only can this be time-consuming and cause considerable inconvenience and expense, but it can also have unfortunate consequences should not all of the estate be traced or, for example, unexpected creditors later appear on the scene.

It goes without saying that it is in your own interests to keep your financial affairs in order throughout your lifetime and know where everything is kept. You will almost certainly have to refer to individual documents at various stages.

If you cultivate the habit of keeping files of all the different documents and certificates or records of where they are, life will be much easier for you, too.

The lists below are by no means

comprehensive. Equally some items may not be relevant. But they should prove helpful in checking on the kind of things your executors will need - and where they are - when you die.

You should leave a note AND tell your next of kin or executor where to find specific items and give all relevant information and essential contacts, as follows:

PERSONAL ITEMS
- THE WILL
- Birth certificate
- Marriage certificate
- Divorce grant
- Driving licence
- Passport
- National Insurance number
- Social Security number
- TV licence
- Place of work
- Contact at work
- Solicitor
- Religious adviser

FINANCIAL ITEMS
- Bank accounts
- Building society accounts
- Post Office accounts
- Pension book

- Pension plans
- Insurance policies
- Stocks and shares
- Savings certificates
- Premium bonds
- Private club accounts
- Safety deposit boxes
- List of valuables
- Insurance certificates/valuations
- Bills paid
- Bills unpaid
- Hire purchase agreements
- Rental agreements
- Court orders
- Money owed
- Money owing
- Accountant
- Insurance broker
- Tax office
- Tax number

NOTE: The more details you can give on your financial affairs, the better. These will include contacts and telephone numbers of people who look after your money and investments, as well as certificates, paying-in and drawing-out books and any other relevant paperwork.

GENERAL ITEMS
- Relatives to contact
- Friends to contact
- Groups or societies to contact
- Donation of organs
- Funeral arrangements
- Other instructions not in the will

REMEMBER... Once you are dead, you will not be around to tell people where everything is or what special instructions you want carried out. So you MUST let someone know... before it's too late.

Index